Maia

Digital Stories

The Poetics of Communication

Foreword by Antonino Saggio

Birkhäuser – Publishers for Architecture
Basel • Boston • Berlin

Original manuscript in English

A CIP catalogue record for this book is available from the Library of Congress, Washington D.C., USA.

Deutsche Bibliothek Cataloging-in-Publication Data

Engeli, Maia:
Digital stories : the poetics of communication / Maia Engeli. Foreword by Antonino Saggio. - Basel ; Boston ; Berlin : Birkhäuser, 2000
  (The IT revolution in architecture)
  Einheitssacht.: Storie digitali <engl.>
  ISBN 3-7643-6175-1
  ISBN 0-8176-6175-1

This work is subject to copyright. All rights are reserved, whether the whole or part of the material is concerned, specifically the rights of translation, reprinting, re-use of illustrations, recitation, broadcasting, reproduction on microfilms or in other ways, and storage in data bases. For any kind of use permission of the copyright owner must be obtained.

Original edition:
Storie digitali (Universale di Architettura 64, collana diretta da Bruno Zevi; La Rivoluzione Informatica, sezione a cura di Antonino Saggio).
© 1999 Testo & Immagine, Turin

© 2000 Birkhäuser – Publishers for Architecture, P.O. Box 133, CH-4010 Basel, Switzerland.
Printed on acid-free paper produced of chlorine-free pulp. TCF ∞
Printed in Italy
ISBN 3-7643-6175-1
ISNB 0-8176-6175-1

9 8 7 6 5 4 3 2 1

Contents

Fear of the Demo? *Foreword by Antonino Saggio*	5
1. Messages: Screens are Small – Ideas are Big	7
The Ephemeral Aspect of Digital Data	10
Behind the Screen	14
Passing Messages	15
2. Architecture: Rooms are Part of Life	19
The Seven Rooms	24
3. Let's Talk Visible	27
Graphicspeak	27
Tsunami of Data	30
Visible Language	32
The Visible Language Workshop – VLW	33
4. Images: Touching the Soul	39
Reading	39
Writing	42
Light	44
Animation	46
Construction	48
Deconstruction	49
5. Stories: Documentary, Poetry, Fiction, Comics, Film, Advertising	51
Communication	51
Knowledge	51
Genres: Documentary, Poetry, Fiction	54
Media: Comics, Film, Advertising	55
The Audience	59
Abstraction and Closure	60
6. Hyperdocument: Creating the Mesh	63
virtualhouse.ch	63
Hypertext	65
Links – Where do they lead to?	67
The New Reading and Writing	71
7. Information Spaces: New Spheres to Explore	75
Views	77
Activities	79
Attention and Enjoyment	80
8. Learning: Discoveries Beyond the Frontier	83
Learning has to be a Fun, Creative, Social and Cultural Activity	83
Architecture, Computers and Learning	85
Narratives, Networks and Architecture	87
Digital Environments for Learning	90
Bibliography	92

I would like to thank Nino Saggio for giving me the chance to write this book. Many thanks go to Prof. Gerhard Schmitt, who has provided the opportunities to work on the interesting projects this book is based upon. Thanks to Bige Tuncer, Urs Hirschberg, Eric van der Mark, Patrick Sibenaler, Fabio Gramazio, Cristina Besomi and Arley Kim for their careful reading and valuable comments on the manuscript. Thanks to all the students in the 1997–98 courses "Raumgeschichten" and "Hyperräume" for their great work and ideas, from which most of the illustrations in this book are drawn. Their teachers were Cristina Besomi, Fabio Gramazio, Maria Papanikolaou, Patrick Sibenaler, Cornelia Quadri, Mark Rosa, Roelof Speekenbrink, Rasmus Joergensen, and Markus Lüttin. The names of the students can be found at the Internet site: http://alterego.arch.ethz.ch/ under the courses of the Academic Year 1997–98. Andreas Weder, with support from Patrick Sibenaler and Mark Rosa, created the inspiring, digital environment for the courses.

Malgorzata Miskiewicz-Bugajski (MMB) did the graphical layout, selected the images and composed them for this book. She has devoted a lot of time to this task and was a big help in the overall process of writing and illustrating the book.

Fear of the Demo?

Preface by Antonino Saggio

The old idea of the computer was linked to incommunicability. People who knew how to use it were cloaked in an aura of technical mystique. They tapped out abstruse codes and, as if by miracle, figures, tables, equations and graphs appeared. They wore white coats and, preferably, thick glasses. Above all, they spoke almost no ordinary language, so the others just had to lie back and wait for the results. But, nowadays, the others have become players.

The revolution came in three stages, all three generated from below. The first was linked to the birth of the personal computer. In the mid Seventies, the "techno" arm of the period's counterculture showed that instead of being the exclusive prerogative of elite groups (military, financial, academic and professional), the power of computing could be extended to the masses. Personal computers sprang up from garages, lofts and kitchens turned into workshops, to gradually conquer the mass market. And even the giants were forced to produce an object they had scorned for years.

The second revolution was centred on the struggle between uncommunicability / communicability. The first personal computers were based on an industrial, mechanical language. It was assertive and certain. You had to write *exactly* what you wanted to do. An error in punctuation, a comma instead of a full stop, blocked communication between user and machine. The language that spread from 1984 was instead metaphorical. Communication was solved through "images".

Of course, in the information era, the possibility of condensing dozens and dozens of bits of data in significant blocks - images, in fact - is the key. We have already talked about the fact that the rhetorical figure has once again taken center place because the problem has been officially posed of communicating rapidly in an inter-connected, directed, anti-objective and anti-assertive fashion.

The third step was based on the creation of a new *modular* programming language (i.e. that can function through independent parts), *multi-platform* (that can control different computer types and models), *multimedia* (that can use digital data that describe different outcomes: sounds, film, three-dimensional objects, texts etc.) and, last but not least, easy to learn and manage.

The first large-scale launch was *Hypertalk*, while the language most widely used today is HTML (Hyper Text Markup Language), which, as is well known, was the basis of the worldwide Internet revolution. William Atkinson and *Hypercard* in the first case, Mark Andreesen and Netscape in the second, were the drivers of a wave of change that has affected millions of people.

6

And now to come to this book. What is the fundamental question being asked here?

We could say that *Digital Stories, The Poetics of Communication* starts out from an assumption. Communication is one of the centers of the information era because it is a "structural" component of today's society. Given that information is the primary commodity, the capacity for transmission, we could say "distribution", is the necessary consequence. Today more than ever, without communication you could do almost literally nothing. The desire to know, to understand, to be able to participate in decisions is more and more widespread. The information society, even if it also hides worrying Orwellian scenarios, can lead to clearer and more extensive participation. The process towards communication is in any case an unstoppable trend. The problem for everyone is, once again, "how".

Communication demands, for architects in general and especially for the increasing ranks of specialists who deal with the "communication project", an increasing degree of awareness.

It is on this search for awareness that the author works. She highlights, first of all, the structure of the data, the medium of the screen, the method of language by images, and sequential and hypertext sequences.

The thesis underlying the various materials is that communication also opens up a new "narrative" space, in tune with a general interest for architecture that re-discovers multiple layers of meaning. Architecture itself appears less and less as an objective fact, as a functionalistic and mechanistic *Sachlichkeit*, and becomes more and more what it is, a fact of communication.

Maia Engeli can interweave this communicative component into the architecture-computer relationship for many reasons. The first, not insignificant one, is a personality open to the communicative and literary dimension that broadens strictly technical knowledge. In addition, the fact of having frequented Nicholas Negroponte's Media Lab, and having been in contact with an inspirer of messages like Muriel Cooper, together with experimentation conducted both alone and with her students in Zurich, certainly makes her a point of reference.

Indeed, the book itself is an example of communication, even just leafing through it, reading the captions, flipping through the bottom of the pages with images that make up a film. Underlying this effort is the great lesson of pragmatism. Ideas must be put into practice, be experimented, become things. John Dewey indicated "learning by doing", "demo or die" is Negroponte's formula. A formula which, from the kids who invented the first personal computers in the seventies to this book, travels like a challenge towards more abstract, theoretical, cerebral cultures. In brief, experimentation, even and above all in communication is a must. "Don't Fear the Demo" is the encouragement we need.

saggio@axrma.uniroma1.it

1. Messages: Screens are Small – Ideas are Big

Screens are very small windows onto the digital universe. Have you ever been annoyed by the fact that the screen is already cluttered after you have opened only a few windows? What fits on a screen – let's take a big one with a diagonal size of 21 inches and 1280 x 1024 pixels resolution – is less than what can be printed on a postcard. This is true if we just count the dots and do not consider the dimensions; since the pixels on a screen are five times as big as the dots on a postcard, you get a larger display area on a screen but not a bigger resolution.

How Much Space is Needed?

If you were in Bilbao visiting the new Guggenheim Museum by Frank Gehry, how many postcards would you write to a friend to let him participate in your experience? Would one be enough? The most representative one, showing the silhouette and the shiny materials from the outside? Maybe two – one from the outside and one from the inside? Or four from the outside, showing different points of view so that your friend can imagine the volumetric composition? How many would you really need to communicate the experience of the spaces, the fascination of the interior, the sensation of light and materials, the complete architectural oeuvre? It may be cheaper and more effective to buy your friend a ticket to Bilbao, because no number of postcards can equal the real experience.

Only built architecture can be visited physically. Projects in the making, architecture in the state of virtuality, have to be presented to the clients and future visitors with other means. Moreover, the communication of ideas has to be convincing because a lot of time and money still needs to be invested to turn a project into a physically real creation. The client needs a chance to identify with the future building, a chance to imagine the planned physical reality, and a way to relate current needs with the designed spaces.

Imaginary postcards of Frank Gehry's Guggenheim Museum in Bilbao. Photos Mark Rosa.

Why do we have to consider screens at all? Architects can draw, they can build models, and they can talk. Displaying information on a screen does not seem to be a necessity.

However, there are a number of reasons why screens have gained importance and it is not mainly to replace any of the traditional means of communication. We cannot deny that screens have become very important and prominent devices for information delivery. Banking and money transferring is

done via screens. The latest world-wide news is shown on TV screens. Offices can hardly exist anymore without computers and monitors connected to them. In train stations and airports even the most computer illiterate traveller has to learn to read important information from screens. And, because of the Internet, people increasingly acquire computers and screens for their private households.
Screens are windows onto a variety of different themes. Although

The Tamagotchi, *the most successful computer pet. Like any digital data it needs care or it will die.*

they show very little at a time, the more you travel the more you can discover of the endless world behind the screen. It is a multifaceted, colorful, perpetually changing universe full of ideas and life. The attractiveness and the possibilities for mental immersion are quite impressive, as is pointed out in books like *Life behind the Screen* by Sherry Turkle (Turkle, 1995), or *Hamlet on the Holodeck* by Janet Murray (Murray, 1997).

The Ephemeral Aspect of Digital Data

Anything you look at on a computer screen has to exist as digital data. Some of the information gets created digitally, for example architectural projects that are modelled with a CAD tool. Other information may be imported from the physical realm, for example photographs of existing buildings.

Some data exist only for a few seconds, like images from a live camera. Other data may be stored for a longer time, but even long-living digital information has a relatively short life span compared with physically stored data. Electronically stored data may get lost due to electronic or physical reasons, programs that accidentally overwrite important information, magnetic influences from the environment, the physical destruction of the device, or the loss of the storage device.

meal	candy	shit	flush
glad	angry	sick	sleep

Even if the data is not lost, it can become useless because there may be no more programs that can read it.

Does this mean that nothing in the world behind the screen can get really old? Well – it has to be kept alive. If data is left alone it will die. Any data that is in use and gets updated regularly will stay alive as long as it remains relevant. Websites are a case in point. Pages that once held relevant data may look dated after a while. Links may not work anymore and other information is not as up-to-date as it should be. Many bad examples can be found on the World Wide Web. Such sites may have been created by an enthusiastic employee, who did the first, very elaborate version and then, because of lack of time and interest, the project is forgotten.

Digital data needs care, like a *Tamagotchi*. From time to time somebody has to control the integrity, the relevance, the actuality and the correctness. For physical buildings maintenance is a necessity. Frequent cleaning is important to keep the place in a hygienically safe condition. The chimney has to be controlled regularly to avoid the danger of fire, the walls have to be repainted from time to time, the roof may need repairs after a storm, the different appliances need to be replaced from time to time, and numerous other examples could be mentioned here. Whoever owns a house knows

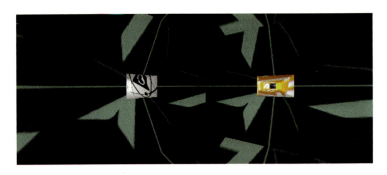

Medienkörper *by Patrick Sibenaler is a follow-up to* TRACE; *the user can move through the ideas in the system, thereby creating his own body of thoughts as seen in these views.*

about the effort that is necessary to keep it in good shape. The same process of constant regeneration is also required to keep digital constructs in a pleasant condition.
What we like about historical buildings is the patina they acquire, the layer representing age and showing the traces of a long life. Does the digital world also have this kind of memory, one that can show the traces left behind and surfaces gaining a depth that can reveal past events? This is where big differences emerge between the digital and the physi-

cal world. The digital world has been thought out by humans, so any desired qualities have to be specifically implemented. If desired, a program could be written that creates digital patina. A number of different projects have looked at the possibilities of creating history in the digital world. *Xanadu*, an infinite project by Ted Nelson, was a very ambitious project to create a global hypertext system that would make all the knowledge accessible from any point and would record all the changes made to the global body of knowledge (see Wolf, 1995). *TRACE*, an installation for the Museum of Contemporary Art in Tokyo, dealt with the theme "Archaeology of

the Future City" in a digital, future city. *TRACE* is a system that records the paths of the users in the digital world and displays them graphically in a three dimensional digital model. Everyone who visits *TRACE* leaves some marks in the system, a history of their movements (Wenz, 1996). The Internet Archive (http://www.archive.org/) is the most thorough attempt to preserve the history of digital data. It is run by a non-profit organization founded by Brewster Kahle. The mission is to collect and store public material from the Internet such as World Wide Web pages, Netnews and downloadable software. The archive will help historians, researchers, scholars, and others to access its extensive collection of data (reaching ten terabytes), and ensure the longevity of this information (Kahle, 1996)

Historical preservation is not a principal characteristic of the digital universe and will never be comparable to the traces that mark the physical environment. In the physical world it is actually very hard to erase things permanently, whereas in the digital world data often gets lost by accident without leaving the slightest trace.

Behind the Screen

Atoms and bits, physical versus digital data is also a favorite theme of Nicholas Negroponte (Negroponte, 1995, p. 11). Transportation, processing, and interaction are the real strengths of the digital realm. Whenever digital data are accessed, processes are triggered to deliver data or to create the desired information on the fly. The electronic version of the Swiss train schedule is a good example for information delivery versus calculation. To receive the schedule between

Zurich and Bern no calculation is needed; this information can be retrieved directly from the database, because it is not necessary to change trains on this journey. However, travelling from Zurich to the Matterhorn is very complicated and a number of possibilities exist for this journey; the system therefore has to process different information to find the best combinations.

The world behind the screen also has a life of its own. Many autonomous processes work invisibly in the background to produce and modify data. Some of what these processes are doing may never attract a person's conscious attention. For example, thousands of computers at the nodes of the Internet automatically exchange and co-ordinate addresses with each other, so that data can be transmitted between them with maximum speed and reliability.

Numerous great ideas from the digital world become visible through the screen. Screens can take on different forms, like the very large projections in movie theatres, the TV screen, and the usual monitor that one finds on a desktop. Very small screens can be found in VR helmets. There is a pair of them, one for each eye to create the three dimensional sensation. 3D shutter glasses or polarizing glasses can also produce this illusion, by letting the left and the right eye see a slightly different picture. Sound, tactile interfaces, and physical feedback devices can further enhance the experience. Virtual rides have recently become fashionable. They provide a combination of Virtual Reality projection in front of a roller coaster that stays in place, but makes jerking movements in co-ordination with the visual sensation. Because of the imagery, the physical experience is as sensational as with a moving roller coaster, but the story that is told can be much more fantastic.

Passing Messages

More has to be invented to enhance the interface between ideas and bits. The first computers could only understand a few specific commands. Nowadays, graphical interfaces allow a more intuitive interaction between humans and the digital world.

Nonetheless, it has to be taken into account that the computer "thinks" very differently from

16

Jenseits - *A Story of a Room from Morning to Evening. The different qualities of light are shown and combined with a poetic text. Authors: Marco Denoth, Martin Fuchs.*

humans. The computer does not "understand" things the way we do. To communicate with a computer we must adapt to its language, know the commands to select from the menu, find the buttons to push, or know the words that can be typed in as commands. Computer programs simulate a human understanding. However, they are mere mechanisms specifically implemented by people, which enable the best possible communication between user and computer. The machine does

not understand the meaning of our interactions in a human way, it does not know what the text we are typing is saying, or what the images that we are drawing represent. The machine is blindly juggling with the data we entrust to it. Small screens can reveal views of great ideas. Since architectural

ideas are quite complex, composed of many layers of possible interpretations, the architect is responsible for composing the messages adequately. The challenge of the small screen has to be met when using computers for communication. In addition, a special effort is needed to attract the viewer's attention. There is much that can be looked at in the digital world and viewers often just stop by, glance around, and leave again. Attention is a precious value in a field where information can grow ad infinitum.

The time a viewer spends at a presentation is an indicator of the amount of information that was transmitted. Presentations on the screen need some "holding power" (Turkle, 1995, p. 30), like *computer games* or narratives. They have to

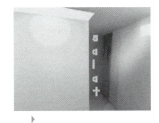

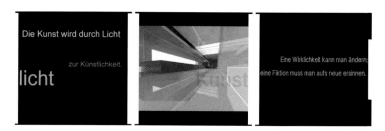

include something that is interesting and engaging, so the game and entertainment industries are good places to look for inspiration even if the goals are not exactly the same. Those industries want to make direct profits by involving the audience. Architects aim for an indirect benefit, they want to build houses, and therefore it may be necessary to know how to reveal great ideas efficiently on a small screen.

2. Architecture: Rooms are Part of Life

> Indeed, architecture finds itself in a unique situation: it is the only discipline that by definition combines concept and experience, image and use, image and structure. Philosophers can write, mathematicians can develop virtual spaces, but architects are the only ones who are the prisoners of that hybrid art, where the image hardly ever exists without a combined activity. (Tschumi, 1994)

Rooms are containers for memories. Memories in turn are important to access new rooms, to feel comfortable because a relationship can be established by connecting the new to the known. Every visit one pays to a room makes it richer and more familiar.

Experiencing a space is a personal and subjective activity. The same room can have a multitude of meanings, as many as the number of people that have visited it and the events that took place in it. Between morning and evening the same room may appear very different. Light and function can change. A breakfast room in the morning can become a room where one writes letters before lunch. In the afternoon it could be the family gathering room and then a tearoom. Later it will become the dining room and afterwards an empty room. Major changes may occur, when a living room is transformed into a party room, or an office space gets rearranged for a reception. Rooms can look different depending on one's mood. On a Monday morning after three weeks' holiday the office is not quite the same as on an ordinary weekday. Rooms look different depending on one's function. The dining room of a restaurant is obviously perceived differently by the waiter compared to the guest.

Similar situations can be found in theatres, lecture halls, or supermarkets.

Time of the day, moods, situations, and circumstances influence one's perception. Even if there are architectural qualities that are independent of subjective perception, the

These renderings show two proposals for the color scheme in a court building in Zürich. Currently the staircase is white, but originally it was painted in Pompeian-Red. Architects and judges wanted to find a compromise. In the dis-

time one spends in a particular room always belongs to a larger event. Architecture itself is seldom the main motivation. A rare exception is the invasion of an exemplary piece of architecture by a class of students, where experiencing architecture is the main reason for the event to happen. The general case is the subjective, individual, unconscious experience of architecture. This situation has to be considered when thinking about portraying spaces that are not built yet.

Clients, the most important audience, have to discover individually interesting qualities in the proposal. They have to discover personally the meaning of the rooms and decide if they are going to like them. In order to reach a conclu-

cussions the stories of the visitors are often mentioned, mostly people in uncomfortable situations, people that getting divorced, or people that may have committed a crime. Renderings by Patrick Sibenaler.

sion, they will try to imagine the rooms, the arrangement of the furniture, different situations in the rooms – alone and with other people, and tasks they want to fulfill in the new environment.

This imagination through virtually experiencing the room by filling it with events, is very important and needs to be supported when presenting a project. Not only the space has to be shown, but also ideas for possible events that will happen in there. Plans, models, drawings and talking are the usual means used to communicate architectural projects. With the computer it is even possible to use three-dimensional, immersive, virtual environments. But still, these almost physical ex-

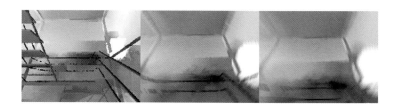

A few frames from the animation Sackgasse *(Dead-End) by Christine Kohler and Astrid Knuth.*

periences are not enough to really appreciate spaces; they have to be filled with life.

Our life consists of sequences of events. Everything we see, learn, and talk about becomes part of a story. That is the way we think and that is the way information should be presented to us (Schank, 1990, pp. 24 - "Storytelling as Understanding", pp. 80 - "Learning Something New"). Stories foster creativity and imaginative thinking, because they can evoke feelings, fantasies and dreams.

Throughout this book, stories about seven rooms are shown. They were provided for the course *Raumgeschichten* (room stories). Seven digital models of different examples of contemporary architecture served as starting points. Some are models of built architecture, others are just projects, some are rooms from apartments, and others are exhibition spaces.

Multiple stories were told about each room. Some are confusing. Some do not tell much about the room, just use it as a model to help create images. Other stories have the form of documentaries, or they just reflect the sequence of the exercises.

The collection of stories written by a multitude of authors has reached a level of complexity, absurdity, and bewilderment where each reader will discover different meanings. Instead of achieving a clearer image while reading the stories, they will raise more questions than answers.

Similar to Italo Calvino's *Invisible Cities* – though not quite at the same level of literary mastery – the collection of stories becomes a space in itself, with a confusing, suggestive, humorous, and poetic character.

> "It cannot be taken for granted that Kublai Khan believed everything Marco Polo said when describing the cities visited on his missions": thus begins an account of travels through cities that cannot be found on any map. [...] Perhaps of the only journey still possible: the one inside the relationship between places and their inhabitants, inside the desires and distress that lead us to live in cities, to make them our element, and to suffer them. (Calvino, 1986)

The Seven Rooms

1. Steinfels. A modern living room, a space that simultaneously serves many purposes; it is a kitchen, a dining room, a library, a living room, a TV room, a playground, a staircase, and sometimes even a party room. The architects are Kaufmann & van de Meer
from Zurich. The Dutch influence from Van de Meer is noticeable in the openness, the lightness, and the experimental, generous character of the space. On both sides of the room, one gets a great view onto the most urban part of Zurich and the Alps in the far distance. The two-story apartment was build on top of an old soap factory, which unfortunately stopped production. Instead of being surrounded by

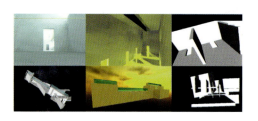

gently perfumed air, the unpleasant smell of the beer brewery on the first floor now penetrates the air from time to time.

2. La Congiunta. The museum for the works of Josephson was designed by Peter Märkli, Zurich. The concrete building is composed of three similar, but differently scaled rooms. The walls have no windows, all the light floods down from the top. The solitary building was built in the rural, hilly territory in the Leventina Valley in the Italian part of Switzerland. The coldness of the closed walls and the fact that there is usually only one or two people visiting the museum at a time emphasizes the solitude of the place.

3. Pavilion. This is a project for an exhibition pavilion on the bank of the Limmat River in Zurich. The design by Maria Papanikolaou was created in a design class at the Master's Program at ETH Zurich in 1996. The interior

space has several different kinds of openings that create varying light situations. The materials are not determined, only color suggestions were made. The blue cube in the center of the space is a particularly dominant object. It turned out to be a provoking element, that triggered ideas for many fascinating stories.

4. *The Kimbell Museum of Fine Arts* in Amon Carter Square Park, Fort Worth, Texas, was designed by Louis I. Kahn for the Art Collection of Mr. and Mrs.  Kimbell. This museum was the last building designed by Louis Kahn (1901–1974) that could be completed under his supervision in 1972. It is renowned for the innovative interaction of natural light, space, and materials. The museum is covered with shell-like concrete vaults. Three courts are cut into the roof, they open the view to the sky and let in different qualities of light. The structural elements in relation with the openings result in an exciting spatial zoning. The Kimbell Museum serves many purposes and allows a wide range of personal impressions of carefully formed interior and exterior spaces to be gathered. (Johnson, 1975, Cummings, 1989, p. 100).

5. Tadao Ando designed this small, concrete, row house in 1976 for a dense urban district in Osaka, Japan. The house has only a few small openings to the outside. It is introverted, organized around a minute courtyard that provides daylight for the surrounding spaces. An open-air bridge that connects the front with the back part of the house runs through the courtyard. Even though it is small and has very few rooms, the house provides a sophisticated composition of spaces and an architectural *promenade* with different views. The vision of a sequence of rooms that fill the space of this house became the starting point for many stories.

6. A digital building specifically designed for the course *Raumgeschichten* by Patrick Sibenaler. It is a simple composition of a half-covered space with a balcony and serves no other purpose than to be a good model for the students to work with. Natural light can be combined with light from numerous predefined artificial light sources. The openness to the outside facilitates the selection of viewpoints for the imaging. The large opening of the space has led to a number of sequences that show how one approaches the building.

7. The young Japanese architect Waro Kishi designed this house in Shimogamo, Tokyo. The basic elements are a steel frame structure and formed cement plates. Unusually for Japanese architecture, privacy is not emphasized, but the interior-exterior relation becomes a major quality of this house. Traditional Japanese architecture as well as the work of Mies van de Rohe influence Kishi's work. His compositions of space and materials are carefully designed masterpieces that show subtle combinations of elements. In many stories, the house was interpreted as a single space, where inside and outside penetrate each other. (Kishi, 1996, p. 72)

The images of the rooms are from the coursework done by the students in the course *Hyperräume* 1998. They were selected and composed by MMB (Malgorzata Miskiewicz-Bugajski).

3. Let's Talk Visible

Written and spoken language is being enhanced with visual means. It becomes more and more common to use pictures, videos and graphics for everyday communication. Digital cameras for video and photography are gaining popularity. Computer tools to create visually appealing layouts and graphics are also being developed and widely used. The tendency towards visible talk is obvious.

Graphicspeak
In his science fiction novel *EON* written in 1985 Greg Bear envisioned graphicspeak, also referred to as picting. The story is about a huge meteorite that enters the earth's orbit in the year 2000. The stone, as the inhabitants of earth call it, returns from the future. It opens a way to the successors of the current human race; a progressive society over five hundred centuries more advanced than the generation currently living on earth. One of the amazing abilities that evolved over this time is graphicspeak. Instead of audible speaking, visible symbols flash between people.
Bear writes:

> The visuals come from pictor torques around their necks, devices which generated and projected the graphicspeak that had developed over the centuries in the Thistledown and in the Axis City. (Bear, 1985, p. 258)

For the old generation of humans it is almost impossible to understand picting:

> Suli Ram Kikura tracted towards Patricia and intercepted the rapid pictings of a man whose skin had the sheen of black hematite. The man apologized in a few simple picts for his assumption that Patricia knew the highest degrees of graphicspeak. (Bear, 1985, p. 374)

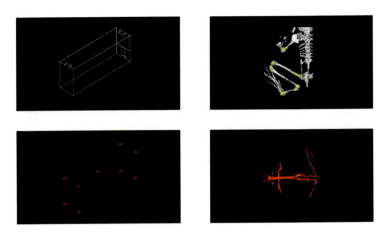

Metamorphose, *a story using analogies by Remo Burkhard and Sascha Vogel.*

One advantage of picting is exemplified during an important testimony before the high ministers:

> "Do we have permission to playback our records and to testify by picting?" Ram Seija gave his permission. In few minutes they became acquainted with the new human occupants of the Thistledown's chambers. Olmy and the frant had managed to record some five hundred individuals on their instruments [...] The picted testimony continued. In less than four minutes, it showed the beginning of the Death and concluded with the spectacle of Earth covered with a thick grey pall of smoke, on the threshold of the Long Winter. (Bear, 1985, p. 338)

Graphicspeak – at its highest perfection – is a very efficient

method of passing information. It is certainly faster than spoken or written language. With graphicspeak it is also possible to pass information that can not be expressed verbally. For example, an overview of a system is better shown with a map, or occurrences that happened over time can be

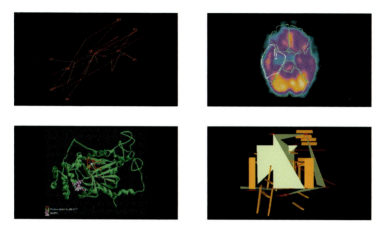

laid out graphically to show how they may have influenced each other. Think of a family tree. Two or three generations back can be explained verbally, but more will become too complex without the help of a graphical representation. Graphics can explain more complex relations in space and time than verbal language is able to do. Therefore, graphic communication can be regarded as a further step in the evolution of the possibilities of communication, which is an evolution of connections that can be drawn.

It is not impossible to learn graphicspeak, in fact our written language has evolved from graphical symbols that once represented objects and actions. Egyptian hieroglyphs are a familiar example. Chinese symbols still contain graphical elements that refer to their meaning.

Linguists are debating the theory that the visible language 'lettere' and the audible language 'lingua' were devoloped independently. Over time, the 'lettere' became weaker and 'lingua' gained importance (Trabant, 1997).

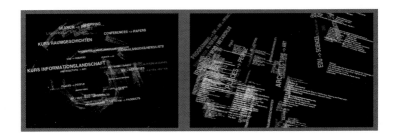

Tsunami of Data

There is a *tsunami* of data that is crashing onto the beaches of the civilized world. This is a tidal wave of unrelated, growing data formed of bits and bytes, coming in an unorganized, uncontrolled, incoherent and cacophony of foam. None of it is easily related, none of it comes with any organization methodology. As it washes up on our beaches, we see people in suits and ties skipping along the shoreline, men and women in fine shirts and blouses dressed for business. We see graphic designers and government officials, all getting their shoes wet and slowly submerging in the dense trough of stuff. Their trousers and slacks soaked, they walk stupidly into the water, smiling – a false smile of confidence and control. The *tsunami* is a wall of data – data produced at greater and greater speed, greater and greater amounts to store in memory, amounts that double, it seems, with each sunset. On tape, on disks, on paper, sent by streams of light. Faster, more and more and more. Now for the good news: There is a dune on the beach. There is a breakwater in the ocean that is clearly emerging in these fleeting moments of the 20th century. The breakwater is indeed breaking up the *tsunami* of data and focusing it in a more organized way to answer our questions and concerns.

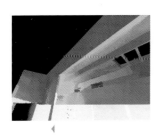

There is a new breed of graphic designers, exhibition designers, illustrators and photographers, whose passion it is to make the complex clear. I call this new breed of talented thinkers Information Architects and this book was created to help celebrate and understand the importance of their work – work which

inspires hope and that as we expand our capabilities to inform and communicate that we will value, with equal enthusiasm, the design of understanding. (Wurman, 1996)

Whenever a new means of communication was invented – like printing, telephony, or film – the next step meant discovering the specific characteristics of the new media. Regarding the book, Murray points out that it took more than fifty years of experimentation to establish such conventions as legible typeface, page numbering, paragraphing, title pages, and chapter divisions (Murray, 1997, p. 28). In the case of highly networked multimedia environments, hard- and software engineers are working on increasing efficiency in technical terms. To shape the new media, Brenda Laurel says that it is important to give control to those who understand human beings, human interaction, communication, pleasure, and pain (Laurel, 1991).

Multimedia is an efficient means of communication. It is engaging because it addresses multiple senses simultaneously. The more of our senses are involved in receiving information the better we can concentrate. Any sense that is not busy with receiving information regarding a specific message is open to distraction from other sources. Moreover, the combination of verbal and visual concepts into a visible language has a potential beyond increasing the efficiency of perception.

The Sofa, *a story that combines the rooms of the Kimbell Museum of Fine Arts with a story by Daniil Charms and Music by Keith Jarret. Authors: Marta Zunino and Philipp Bessire.*

Most people find it difficult to understand purely verbal concepts. [...] We employ visual and spatial metaphors for a great many everyday expressions. [...] We are so visually biased that we call our wisest men visionaries! (McLuhan, 1967)

Visible Language

A visible language will allow for faster delivery and reading of information, which is crucial as accessibility is increasing. A visible language will ease the act of working with complex interrelated information, because it contains the means not only to reveal single messages but also the connections between single pieces and overviews of collections of information.

A visible language goes beyond pure visualization. Visualizations are representations of objects, spaces, relations, or structures, like renderings of a planned building.

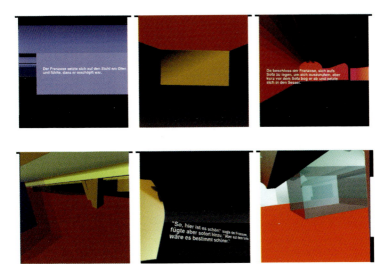

The purpose of visualizations is to reveal information directly related to the object in question. A visible language on the other hand includes a semiotic use of visual representations. A visible language can consist of designed text, "talking" images, or a combination of both. Layout (formats, proportions, grids), typography (typefaces, typesetting), imagery (concrete to abstract signs, icons, symbols), visual identity (appearance), sequencing, animation (dynamics of display), color, and texture are important aspects of a visible language. Metaphors, cognitive models, aesthetic appearance, and effective interaction are the qualities that have to be considered for a visible language in the digital realm (Greenberg).

The Visible Language Workshop – VLW

The VLW (Visible Language Workshop) at the MIT (Massachusetts Institute of Technology) was founded in 1975 by Muriel Cooper. Muriel Cooper was an award winning designer, who has produced over 500 books, the

well-known Bauhaus Book (Wingler, 1969) among them. In 1985 the VLW was among the eleven groups that were merged to become the MIT Media Lab.

In 1994 Muriel Cooper died at the age of 68. The VLW became the Aesthetics and Computation Research Group under John Maeda in 1995. The rest of this chapter is devoted to the VLW, where I spent two years as a student and researcher, from 1992 to 1994.

The research at the VLW originated in printing as the media for visual communication. The design research in this area was the foundation for exploring new possibilities as they arose from new technological achievements. David Small formulated the goal of the group as follows:

> The overall plan was to investigate the intersections of visual communication, design research, and artificial intelligence. Of major concern were the qualitative graphic filtering of information in a dynamic, interactive, and expressive multimedia environment, the relationship of traditional design knowledge to electronic media, and the evolution of a new graphics vocabulary to delineate synthesized static and dynamic characteristics (Cooper, Small, 1996).

Demo or Die – the Media Labs parlance – was most important for the VLW, because everything here was visible. Every student had to give several demos a week, which happened in the *open working space* of the lab. Some of the visitors were so impressed that they remained speechless, others became really interested and asked a lot of questions. The most exciting moments were when demos could be given to famous artists, like Peter Gabriel or Laurie Anderson.

The demos we were most proud of were the demos on The Big Guy, the world's biggest screen at that time, with a resolution of 2000 x 6000 pixels. This amount of screen real-estate was challenging. It is so big that one cannot see all of it at a glance, but it provides a lot of space to spread out information. For example the News-Demo displayed a beautiful satellite image of the whole world, the colors enhanced, all clouds removed, over the 2000 x 6000 pixels. This image served as the basis on which to place headlines of the world-news: important ones were larger, old ones were fading, a color-coding scheme helped to structure the information further. The news was always up to date, directly drawn from a news-wire link and organized automatically on the display. The headlines were linked to the articles, including images and videos if available. The articles appeared right next to the headline using elaborate algorithms to calculate the transparency needed so that the text is readable, but does not obscure too much of the context.

Maps were important parts of many prototypical applications. Maps allow a view of the form and structure of the environment, they help people to imagine a context more clearly, and they enhance the understanding of relations. Maps can be drawn for physical environments as well as abstract information spaces. One map demo was run on a Connection Machine which, in 1993, was one of the most advanced massively-parallel supercomputers with 65536 processors. The high calculation speed was used to move through layers of information. In smooth transitions, information appeared and disappeared, parts were enhanced, while others were blurred, resulting in a pleasant sensation of floating through a space of changing focus, showing an appropriate amount of information at each time.

A simulation of paper and watercolor was also done on the connection machine. Each processor of the parallel-computer reflected a fiber of the paper. This straightforward approach resulted in very realistic simulations of different papers and different water-color techniques. Oil-paint could be simulated with these algorithms by introducing gravity instead of dissolution in any direction. After some testing, the algorithms were translated for smaller computers and integrated

Watercolor and Oil-paint Simulation by David Small, VLW, Media Lab MIT (Copyright MIT Media Lab, 1990).

with other prototypes of tools for expressive, dynamic information design.

Cartoons were another focus at the VLW. Steve Lebrande had developed a system to interpolate between different expressions of a cartoon character. The system was fed with three to five examples drawn by an artist. Initially it would generate the in-between states in a naïve way and had to be trained to generate the most sophisticated solutions. The example in the demo showed Garfield, because Paws – the Garfield Company – was sponsoring this research. A happy Garfield from front, a sad Garfield from the side, … with sliders one could change the expression and move between different views. The whole

face would change when Garfield closed his eyes, opened his mouth, or became angry (Lebrande, 1993). The behavior was touching. People were so fascinated that they forgot that there was a computer in the back generating the images.

The *Baby Crying* demo was very disturbing to the other researchers

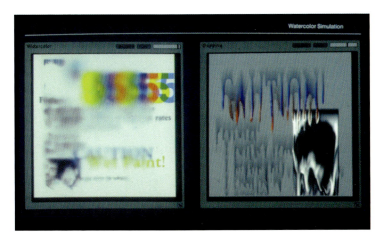

in the lab. It was a demonstration of expressive typography, using a combination of text and sound. The shape of the written word "Aaah!" dynamically reflected the sound of the crying baby. A very impressive demonstration, but since that crying sound had to be played at each demo, once or twice a day, it really got on the nerves of the people working in the same room.

These are just a very few examples of the creative and productive environment that was generated under Muriel Cooper's influence. I got to know her when she was 64. Muriel Cooper was a lively, energetic person, with a special aura. After her sudden death at 68, Richard Wurman dedicated the book *Information Architects* to her. He wrote, "I believe Muriel had wings …", wings that create the wind of change, wings of a peace dove, wings to fly towards new visions, wings of triumph, wings that encourage her students (Wurman, 1996). Muriel was neither a programmer nor an ambitious computer user, but she had this steadily expanding vision of how computer interfaces and their visible language should evolve along with the new media. The same rigor that she had applied to

printed media in the past created the drive to search for approaches to display information using digital media. Artificial intelligence, dynamic graphics, sound, and the transition from 2D to 3D were important aspects in the perpetual search for a humanly appropriate display of information. Muriel Cooper passed her drive for aesthetic innovation to many generations of students, motivating them by her experience of a lifetime of progress from print to digital media, an immense quest for improvement, and a strictness in respecting achieved qualities. No compromises that undermined achievable aesthetic qualities were acceptable to Muriel Cooper. To meet high standards of graphical quality was a must. Typefaces and lines had to be anti-aliased. Colors had to be selected carefully from the Munsell color space (Munsell, 1923), for which a special tool was implemented at the VLW.

Muriel Cooper's ideas were always on the edge between pushing the possibilities to the maximum and new desires stemming from the latest technological inventions. It was hard to create something that could meet her expectations, but nonetheless she created an inspiring and motivating atmosphere among her group of students.

4. Images: Touching the Soul

Images and Text reveal information differently. A knowledge of the difference helps to combine them appropriately for each specific message.

> Pictures are *received* information. We need no formal education to "Get the message." The message is instantaneous.
>
> Writing is *perceived* information. It takes time and specialized knowledge to decode the abstract symbols of language.
>
> When pictures are more abstracted from "reality" they require greater levels of *perception*, more like words.
>
> When words are bolder, more direct, they require lower levels of perception and are received faster, *more like pictures*.
>
> (McCloud, 1993, p. 49)

Reading

The reading of images differs in a fundamental way from reading a text. A sentence is read as a linear sequence from beginning to end. It would not make sense the other way round. The succession of the words forms the meaning. Images, on the other hand, do not have an inherent way they should be looked at. One can start at any point and move one's gaze in any direction at free will.

Sentences can be used to make logical, rational statements. Images touch the sensual, emotional perception and their interpretation by the viewer is less predictable. There are exceptions to this general categorization. Poets can write texts that touch our deepest feelings; they can make us laugh and cry just with words. Yet, it needs a certain amount of text to evoke such responses, responses that could be triggered by a single image. The visual display of rational, statistical information with

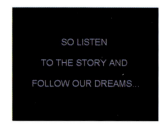 

Have You Had Enough Excitement Today? *story by Bianca von Schweppenburg and Monika Meyenberg.*

charts, diagrams, or graphs are examples where images are utilized to make very clear statements. In combination, words and text can unfold a fascinating tension due to the ambiguous duality of being rational and emotional, precise and vague at the same time.

Words can be employed to focus the interpretation of an image by reducing the possible meanings. The image of an

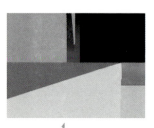

old house at dusk combined with the word "dream!" is a clear message that you should think about something beyond current reality, something imaginative and pleasing. In any case, you do not have to be concerned about the desolate state of the house, its present inhabitants, or any other prob-

41

BE A CAVEMAN

BE A BUTTERFLY

BE IN DREAMS

JUST BE

lems related to it. Just relax and "dream"! Images can illustrate a text and reveal visual information that cannot be described with sentences. Images can also change the meaning of a text. Imagine the word "dream!" underneath the image of a dark room inside an old house filled with dust, a mess of old furniture, spider webs, and maybe some traces of a fight. In such a combination, the meaning of the word dream will be interpreted rather as nightmare.

Combining images and text is a tightrope walk between narrowing and broadening the possible interpretations. There is much freedom and conscious choices have to be made to produce the appropriate effect.

Nightmare *story by Roman Sokalski.*

Writing

To write text is straightforward, we have learned that at school and trained for many years. By comparison very little is taught on how to create adequate images. There are many ways to produce images, especially with the digital tools available nowadays and the new possibilities that are constantly being developed. Choosing the right tool becomes a task in itself. The major categories for software tools are drawing, painting, constructing, rendering, and animating. For each category, numerous different programs exist. Every one of them has its strengths and weaknesses, which will influence the expression of the pictures that can be produced. The tools are the media used to design the message.

Images should be used to produce subjective messages, whose intention is to impose the relevant aspects on the viewer. In the case of architecture, this means that the architect, as the author of an image, has to take responsibility for the message that is communicated, the architect has to make the choice and consider the aspects that have to be emphasized.

The image is not the architecture, it is the message. An image can show aspects that would not be noticed in the real building. In a realistically rendered picture, feelings that are evoked in a room may not be perceived. Images are

not just pictures of a digital model, they fulfill a higher task, which is to transmit selected information to the spirit, the soul and the body of the reader.

When producing images of architectural projects using the computer, three-dimensional digital models are usually the starting point from which more illustrative imagery can be generated with different techniques. When creating specific messages about rooms it is important to know about the characteristic qualities of the different possibilities and the aspects that can be emphasized. We have explored four possibilities in our courses. The rendering and the animation approaches looked at rooms without changing the geometry, while the constructive and the deconstructive approaches interfered with the three-dimensional form of the models. Different teachers, whose intentions are outlined in the next four sections, taught the different possibilities.

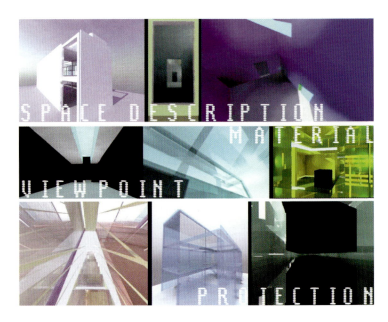

Pictures produced by focussing on light, material, and view. Teacher: Patrick Sibenaler. Composition: MMB.

Light

Patrick Sibenaler showed that rendered objects can be interpreted in different ways. The main parameters – light, material, and view – may support the nature of an object, work against it, reveal new information, and add or negate aspects of the object. Light is of great importance in architecture. The admiration of the sun god Ra dictated the orientation of old Egyptian temples. The metaphorical use of sunlight can be seen in colored church windows from the Middle Ages. Integration of artificial light in the design has become popular in contemporary architecture, as can be seen in buildings by Jean Nouvel, and Toyo Ito. Materials

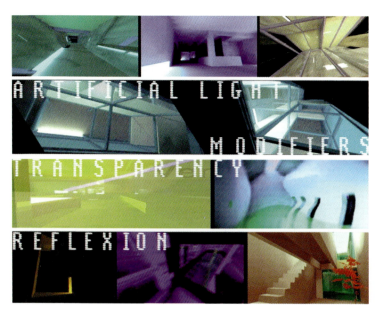

determine optical, haptic and acoustic characteristics. However, only the optical qualities of materials are influential for the visual representation of a space, mainly color, transparency, surface finish and reflection. Perspective and framing persuade the observer. Photographic possibilities (framing, zoom, and focal length) can be complemented with types of projections not available in photography, for example cylindrical, 360-degree, or sphere projections. From rendering the geometry in daylight situations, different seasons or atmospheres, one can move on to work actively with light as a space-defining design element to support the legibility of a space or a design idea.

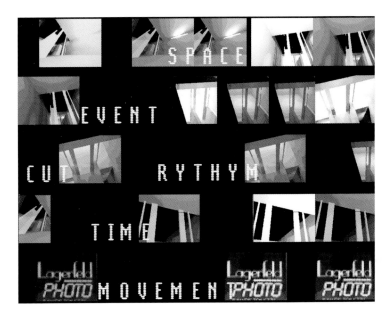

Illustrations composed of still frames from animations. Teacher. Fabio Gramazio. Composition: MMB.

Animation

Animations are sequences of rendered pictures. Sequences are defined by Roland Barthes in *Structural Analysis of Narratives* as: "A logical succession of nuclei bound together by a relation of solidarity: the sequence opens when one of its terms has no solitary antecedent and closes when another of its terms has no consequences."

Sequences generate emotions. The potential of animation, as described by Fabio Gramazio, is the perceivable field between the real geometry of the space, the event, and the movement that can be described using the motion of the camera.

The final meaning of any sequence is dependent on the relation space/

event/movement. By extension, the meaning of any architectural situation depends on the relation S E M. The composite sequence SEM breaks the linearity of the elementary sequence, whether S, E, or M. (Tschumi, 1994)

The structure and flow of the sequence, as well as the cut are important when composing longer sequences. The cut allows the introduction of time as a determining parameter to break with the classical linear perception.
Animations do not mainly have to concentrate on high-quality realistic renderings, but rather on well-structured sequences with a well-controlled meaning.

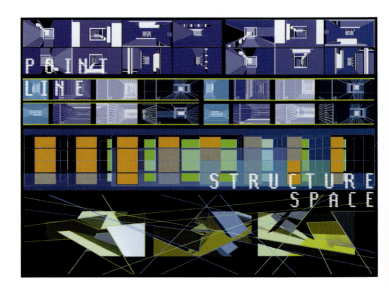

Interpretations resulting from constructing new elements in a given space. Teacher: Cristina Besomi. Composition: MMB.

Construction

For the construction approach Cristina Besomi introduced a strategy of increasing the dimensions of elements that are placed inside the space. A tactic of filling the space with interpretations, so that when, finally, the walls are taken away, the definition is stripped and only the meaning remains. Starting with points, one can mark special places, produce traces, and increase the density of the atmosphere in certain areas of a space. Lines can be introduced to show connections, to indicate directions of movements and views, and to produce grids that reveal a hidden structure. Introducing faces results in separate areas. Finally, by adding three-dimensional objects tangible bodies occupy the space.

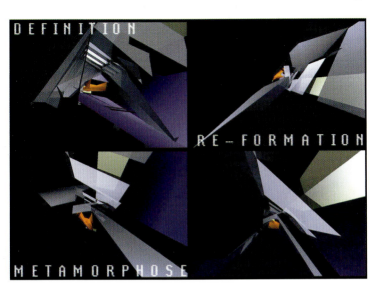

Pictures from the deconstruction approach. Teacher: Maria Papanikolaou. Composition: MMB.

Deconstruction

Contrary to constructing new elements in space Maria Papanikolaou showed that the deconstructing approach can be used to create a metamorphosis from a given to a desired space. The new space is a deformation and fragmentation of the old one, thereby breaking the logic of the structure of the original model. The changed space gains significance, by redefining the spatial relations of the elements in a balancing act between the old and the new and between deconstruction and reconstruction. A deconstructivist attitude respects what is given and transforms it into something new. It does not destroy but expands existing ideas.

Through our education, we are conditioned to believe that text is

the most trustworthy means of representing knowledge. There is a fear that images may not be precise and conclusive enough. We are trained to work with facts, which is obviously shortsighted in times when communication networks have turned global interconnectivity into a popular theme. We have to learn to deal with complex information where answers are not just right or wrong, but may be something in-between. Linear processes are replaced by dynamic systems, life is less about answers and more about one's position and behavior within the surrounding environment. Solutions are not just answers but pieces that interface well with a larger system. The kind of thinking that is needed to deal with such challenges is better reflected in images than in text, because images leave the space for interpretation that is necessary to respect the world as a non-deterministic system.

For architects the attitude of respecting the environment as a complex system is self-evident. Good architectural solutions reflect a deep and anticipative understanding of the numerous interrelated influences. Architectural solutions are buildings that contain the rooms for people to live and work in, and interact with the world. Therefore, images have to show more than objective, realistic representations of a room, they can and should reveal subjective interpretations influenced by the carefully chosen tools that were employed to generate them. If the emotional aspect is brought upfront, the image touches on memories and the architecture that is represented becomes part of an imaginative event, a story that will become part of the reader's memory.

4

5. Stories: Documentary, Poetry, Fiction Comics, Film, Advertising

Communication
Stories have a long tradition as a means of revealing and transporting information. Before the written language was invented, stories about things that happened in far away places were told by storytellers and bards. The storyteller and the bard were professions in ancient times that served to connect distant events and also to entertain people. Oral transportation was followed by the written transportation of information. At first, reading and writing was reserved to a few knowledgeable people, but with the advent of the printing press and the ease of mass production, reading became a widespread skill and today it is a requirement. After listening and reading, film and TV added the possibility to reproduce the images of an event. Nowadays it is possible to combine the aural, written and pictorial means of storytelling in one so-called multimedia event. We can also expect to discover possibilities beyond the linear form of stories in the more complex form of the hyperdocument, an aspect that will be explored in the next chapter.

Knowledge
The ability to tell stories is what distinguishes humans from other animals. The narrative form of revealing information is an inherent capability of our brains and fulfills a number of important tasks. Roger Schank developed a theory on stories and intelligence that actually stems from his desire to make computers smarter.

Regarding memory and communication Schank's theory uncovers interesting aspects of stories and why they should be told.

> We need to tell someone else a story that describes our experience because the process of creating the story also

Leventina, *a short, documentary story about the "La Congiunta" Museum by the architect Peter Märkli. Story by Franziska Frieda Manetsch, Alexandre Arthur Clerc and Marc Zamparo*

creates the memory structure that will contain the gist of the story for the rest of our lives. (Schank, 1990, p. 115)

Knowledge is stories and retelling stories helps to preserve the memories. Because we do not store the whole story but only the gist of a story, the memory fades over time and has to be refreshed. Dreams are explained in an interesting way in Schank's theory. Dreams are stories that we create and recreate several times until the outcome is satisfactory. Dreams are a problem-solving mechanism.

People need a context to help them relate what they have heard to what they already know. We understand events in terms of events we have already understood. (Schank, 1990, p. 15)

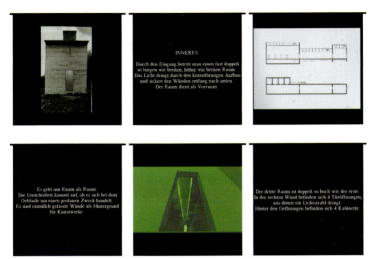

Stories are a valid medium of communication, they allow the listener or reader to connect their own memories at various different points throughout the narrative. Since the audience is always made up of different individuals, one can not predict exactly which part of a story may attract someone's interest. Several possible links to personal experiences have to be provided to capture and hold the audience's attention.

Our memory can only store new information in connection with something that is already known. This is particularly important in the architectural context. The purpose of talking about a project is that the audience finds a way to identify itself with the object that is presented. It is therefore important to

Leventina *(continued from previous page)*.

allow them to make connections to something already known, which does not have to be another building but rather a familiar situation. The clients have to be able to imagine desirable events taking place in the new building, they need input for their dreams. This is the main reason why it is necessary to tell stories about projects. Every architect is in fact doing so when presenting a project, but storytelling is usually not a consciously trained skill even though it is of great importance for the communication of ideas.

Genres: Documentary, Poetry, Fiction

Different genres of narratives reveal information with specific attitudes. Documentaries reveal information in the most objective way, poetry is comparatively subjective, while fiction goes beyond reality and creatively unveils new interpretations. Fiction is usually the most entertaining form, while poetry is emotionally touching, and the documentary tries to reveal information honestly. However, a story that reveals architectural meaning must not necessarily be a documen-

tary, because the goal is to project experiences into the reader's mind. It is easier to accomplish this purpose with fantastic, poetic narratives, since they are more intriguing, they allow for wider, creative interpretations, and they imply that the emotional information is intentionally part of the

  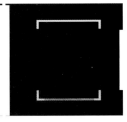

message. The three stories that illustrate this chapter show examples of different genres: *Leventina* is an example of the documentary approach, *Entering* is a poetic story and *Frau Egli* talks about fictitious events.

Media: Comics, Film, Advertising

Besides the genre, the intention and the media are influential in the way a story can be designed. The intention can be entertainment, information, communication, or propaganda. Known media include comics, film, advertising, CD-ROM, or books. Each medium influences the way the message can be formulated and received. An understanding of these implications is an important precondition for making effective use of the possibilities.

Digital stories can have many forms. The simplest ones are sequences of single frames; stories that are more elaborate will include many dimensions and dynamic transitions between them. In our first course, a simple form of digital stories was explored, sequences of relatively small frames that contain images and text. This form was chosen because it is appropriate for the capabilities and limitations of networked computers, where the data transfer speed restricts the amount of information that can be delivered within a reasonable amount of time. This restriction limits the size of the single

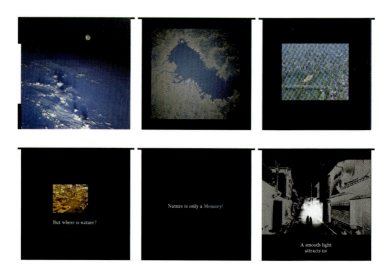

Entering *a story that follows a physical path from the universe into the space and then explores the effects of different seasons. Authors: Simon Weiss and Arley Kim.*

frames to a rather small area of the screen. This constraint is one of the challenges of the new medium. As was described in the first chapter: it is important to be able to express ideas on a small area. The smaller the area the more challenging the task becomes.

The form of telling stories within sequential frames with images and text does not yet have a long tradition that one could learn from. Therefore, we have to look at other examples of storytelling where a combination of media is utilised, like comics, film, and advertising.

The main difference between comics and the digital stories is that comics show many frames on a single page, whereas the digital stories only show one frame at a time. The digital stories are more colorful and the images differ stylistically from comics, but they do not show any overview of a larger

57

part of a story as a page in a comic book does. Thinking of a Mickey Mouse comic, we may have just read that Mickey Mouse is angry with his uncle because they had had an argument. When we arrive at the end of the page we are very curious about how the argument develops. When we turn to the next page, we immediately get an impression of how the story will develop over the next few frames, without having looked at the details. All we need is to see the laughing face of Mickey Mouse in one of the frames and we immediately know that he will feel better in a while. Consequently, we will find ourselves more actively involved in the story because we are forming our own questions of what will happen, while we read on and get the answers. Anticipation is an effective means of keeping the reader's attention. In a medium like the digital stories, where there is no such overview,

58

Entering *(continued from previous page).*

the possibility of anticipation is the result of the sequence of events.
Film combines images, spoken language, and sound. The images are shown at a fast pace so that we perceive a smooth motion until there is a cut. A frame in the digital story would correspond more to the sequence between cuts in a film, than to a single image. Film, like the digital story, always shows one frame at a time. From film, we can learn how excitement and tension can be generated within a sequence so that the effects of curiosity and anticipation come into play. Some films, like Tarantino's *Pulp Fiction*, show very interestingly interwoven stories, where the sequence of the events in the film does not correspond to the sequence in which they happen in the story. Things that happen at the end of the film are shown at the beginning and the sequence switches between parallel stories for a while. From films we can learn how to introduce new dimensions like complexity, tension and depth of meaning into a linear sequence.

Advertising represents a third form we can learn from because they use images and texts to reveal convincing, persuasive information about a product. This attitude makes them particularly interesting since they

Frau Egli *a story that uses a main character and the effects of the smell of a cleaning agent to show weird, distorted perceptions of the space. Author: Thomas Merz.*

not only want to inform and entertain like comics and movies, but are designed to sell a product. When trying to communicate information about architecture a similar attitude is needed. The message has to communicate convincing aspects regarding a product. The Absolut vodka series is an intriguing example of a series that illustrates one product from many points. The advertisement campaign asked contemporary designers to provide illustrative interpretations and resulted in a multifaceted series of visual messages. The breadth of interpretations by the artists is boundless. To allow such a range of views is important for architectural objects as well. To show a product from only one aspect would be very limiting. The goal is to respect the core idea and to show how it could be interpreted in different ways, enabling different individuals to find a mental access as well as to demonstrate a depth and agility of the product that is convincing in various situations.

The Audience

To write a story requires a design process. Many aspects have to be taken into account and combined to create a meaningful, exciting sequence. Stories have a manipulative effect on the reader. An effi-

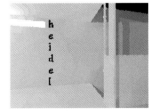

Frau Egli *(continued from previous page)*.

cient way of guiding the reader's involvement is to plan the latter's point of view with care. Will Eisner has convincingly illustrated this aspect in his book *Comics and Sequential Art*. He shows how in the same scene the reader can be in the position of an observer or in the position of a participant, depending on the perspective (Eisner, 1985, p. 90).

Not only the physical but also the mental position of the reader can be influenced. The position can be threatening or distant, it can result in a pleasant involvement or a curious tension. It is the author's achievement to design the situation according to the intention of the story.

Camera position and movement is a very carefully planned aspect of film production. Focus and fuzziness, light and colour, hard and soft lenses are also used to influence the spectator. In film, the point of view and the timing are very well controlled. In comics and digital stories, there is less control, because the timing is less controllable and the environment is less predictable. In architecture, the means of the controlled point of view is even less possible. Openings and paths can guide the visitor. Light and colors can be used in a similar way as they are applied in films to draw attention or to create a special atmosphere.

Abstraction and Closure

A story can never reflect the whole reality, it is always an ab-

straction. When creating a story, this limitation leads to thinking about the possibilities for readers to fill in missing information. The strategy has to consider the parts that can be left open for interpretation by the reader. These situations are created in a suggestive context without exactly formulating everything. These gaps in a story can be very powerful, because the readers will use their own knowledge and fill in familiar situations the author may not know about. The triggering of the right attitude is in the hands of the author, while the information that will fill the gaps stems from other sources. Digital stories as well as comics are composed of as many gaps as frames. Scott McCloud has analysed the phenomena for comics: "This phenomenon of observing the parts but perceiving the whole has a name. It's called closure." He distinguishes six kinds of closure: moment to moment, action to action, subject to subject, scene to scene, aspect to aspect, and non-sequitor (no logical relation) (McCloud, 1993, p. 70).

Digital stories, composed as a sequence of small frames, are a severely restrained form of revealing information with the computer. As has been shown in this chapter, within these restrictions there are numerous ways of expressing ideas.
Many aspects of this new medium

are not fully explored yet. However, it is important to realise that sequential, digital stories are not the ultimate possibility and that we have to consider the hypertextual narrative form as a next step.

6. Hyperdocument: Creating the Mesh

Hyperdocuments are a challenging new way of providing information, challenging for the authors as well as the readers. A hyperdocument allows rich multidimensional information structures to be built where readers can enjoy travelling along various paths. It may also be overwhelmingly complex, leaving the visitors desperately lost in information space.

Virtualhouse.ch

virtualhouse.ch is a hyperbuilding on the Internet that was created by Herzog and de Meuron Architects and our group from the department of architecture and CAAD at ETH Zürich. The project was designed as a contribution to a competition by *ANY Magazine*, New York and Mister Brown from FSB, a German doorhandle company. The competition asked for a rather philosophical examination on the subject of virtuality.

It was not expected that the result would be an Internet installation. After discussing the meaning of virtuality and a wide range of possibilities, the Internet was chosen as the right environment for a virtual house. *virtualhouse.ch* has a simple concept: it is composed of carefully selected images that represent the rooms of the building. On each of the four sides of an image is a connection to the next room. They are one-way connections, you cannot go back where you came from. The house has 29 rooms, which a visitor gets to know well after moving around for a while. It is possible to talk to other people that are present in the same room and the house can consequently be explored together. The following statements describe the main intentions of *virtualhouse.ch*:

virtualhouse.ch is a site on the Internet. The Internet as a digital real-

virtualhouse.ch - *a snapshot from the screen. In the foreground is the room "Thrilling Dreams", the background shows the entry-page and the overview of all the rooms and visitors.*

ity is the obvious place for the virtual house. The Internet is no longer a high-end technical manifestation, it is reality. The Internet superimposes itself on the physical environment with text, images, and sound. The Internet is, thus, a part of our environment.

virtualhouse.ch has no third Cartesian co-ordinate. The spaces are created through images. Their interpretation and associative connections are the architecture. The rooms and the structure are not built from matter, they are built by imagination. They are not created for eternity, they end with the fading of the memories of the visitors.

virtualhouse.ch is an open house, receiving visitors from all over the

virtualhouse.ch - *in this interface, the rooms and their neighbours are shown. Every visitor is allowed to reconfigure virtualhouse.ch with this interface.*

globe, who would never gather in the same physical place. Space is occupied through communication. Visitors transform an empty room into a full one, a quiet space into a loud one. The atmosphere is created interactively through the images and the presence of visitors.

virtualhouse.ch, as any architecture, is concerned with reality. It has to integrate itself in the context of this networked reality, where neither geometry nor gravity dominate any longer. It has to adapt to the vocabulary and codes of the net.

Hypertext

Ted Nelson coined the term hypertext in 1965. Ted Nelson has devoted his work to the development of Xanadu, the absolute Hypertext

system that can connect all the world's online knowledge. The work started at a time when a single computer occupied a whole floor of a building. Nelson had a vision, by connecting all the world's information no copies would be needed, everything would be composed of linked originals. No more need to raise the question of copyrights. Thirty years after the development of *Xanadu* Gary Wolf writes the following:

> It was the most radical dream of the hacker era. Ted Nelson's *Xanadu* project was supposed to be the universal, democratic, hypertext library that would help human life evolve into an entirely new form. Instead, it sucked Nelson and his intrepid band of true believers into what became the longest-running vapourware project in the history of computing – a 30-year saga of rapid prototyping and heart-slashing despair. The amazing epic tragedy. (Wolf, 1995)

The idea to use links to connect different pieces of information that can be followed interactively was the essential feature of the *Memex* – memory Extender – invented by Vannevar Bush already in 1932. The *Memex* represented a private library system containing books, notes, and letters with the possibility of using associative links to connect the items. The first article on *Memex* was published in 1945 under the title: "As We May Think" in *Life* magazine (Bush, 1991).

Hypercard, the program that was shipped with earlier Macintosh Systems, was one of the first wide-spread Hypertext applications. The examples showed analogies to stacks of cards or notebooks. Nowadays, with the experience from Web-pages, the paper-related analogies are almost gone. Hyperdocuments have reached a level of autonomy, but more inventions are still

needed until this form becomes more independent of metaphorical comparisons with the more traditional media.

Many authors and filmmakers have explored the boundaries of books and film to express ideas in a multithreaded way, allowing alternatives and participatory possibilities, but only with the computer did it become possible to write true intertwined hyperstories. Hyperdocuments, multi-threaded stories are the narrative form we want to encourage, as Janet H. Murray points out remembering the development of film during the first thirty years of this century:

> It is important to first identify the essential properties of digital environments, that is, the qualities comparable to the variability of the lens, the movability of the camera, and the editability of the film, that will determine the distinctive power and form of a mature electronic narrative art. (Murray, 1997, p. 68)

Tools that support the creation of hyperfiction are available. They help when designing the single *lexias* (reading units) (Murray, 1997, p. 55) as well as the whole structure. Even though the structure is usually not shown to the reader who is moving from frame to frame, a well designed structure can facilitate its assimilation and allow for the enjoyable reading of the hyperdocument.

Links – Where do they lead to?
The link, the most important feature of hyperdocuments, can be placed at any spot in a text or an image. The reader has to make active choices. Links are "opaque", we cannot see behind them, only the spatial and the temporal context can give an idea of where a particular link will lead. The decision of a reader to follow one link or another is often based on an intuitive rather then a conscious choice.

There are two possible approaches to make the reader feel comfortable when having to choose one link instead of another. One is to construct the whole document in a way that people feel save when moving around. They need to know that they cannot get lost, that they will not miss anything important, and that they can get back easily to a part they liked. The ratio of the time used for navigation compared to the time spent

Examples of "Addition +" and "Analogy =" connections.

reading the content has to be minimized. This ensures that the message can be optimally transmitted. The second way to help the reader with making a choice is by creating meaningful links.

During the course on *Hyperräume*, the follow-up course to *Raumgeschichten*, links were used very consciously to connect the stand-alone linear sequences of the stories into a networked space of information. Four kinds of characteristic links – sequence, analogy, addition, and contrast – were introduced. The signs >, =, +, and # indicated the kind of link so that the reader had the possibility to base the choice on more than just the name of the link.

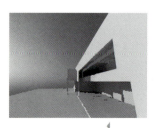

On the Internet, with a little bit of experience, we can recognize what lies behind certain links. We can recognize the entrances to a site,

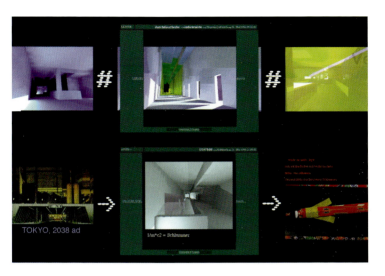

Examples of «Contrast #» and «Sequence >» connections.

links that connect a sequence of documents, links that will reveal more detailed information, others that provide background information or illustrations. Some links will lead to a form where input is required, as in search engines, and others will produce a calculated output in response to the user's input. The worst cases are broken links, which produce frustration in the reader, since his expectations cannot be fulfilled because of a failure in the system. Fortunately, tools to avoid such situations are now being evolved and this will help guarantee the consistency of a hyperdocument.

When he encounters a link, a reader tries to anticipate the connection it establishes. This attitude shown by the reader is an interesting new means for the author of a hyperdocument to use in the composition. It introduces a new level

The Olivenbild *node as a connection between the stories* Dinner *and* Dream On, *node by Alain Dafflon, Elise Guilaume, Katrin Buesser. Composition by MMB.*

to create sensations for the reader. For example: A page with few links differs from a page with many links. Links that lead to expected information may have a calming effect, while links that lead to surprises may stimulate different emotions. Instead of repeating an important statement to emphasize something, a link that connects to the same piece of information can be introduced in multiple locations throughout the document. Links are a powerful means for structuring a hypertext and complex interrelated compositions. Great hypertext writing will require mastery not only in creating the content but also making sensible use of the connections. The composing of great hypertext is an art form and we can expect great hypertext-oeuvres to come into existence.

Fokusierung, *a new node between the stories* Dream On *and* Entering, *node by Daniela Tomaselli and Maximilian Donaubauer. Composition by MMB.*

The New Reading and Writing

Hyperdocuments are changing the act of reading. Reading hyperdocuments requires more than understanding the words and sentences, one also needs to pay attention to the connections. The sequential presentation of information is replaced by choices that lead to different fragments of information. Reading involves an extra task: in addition to reading the content one has to decide where to go next, and keep an overview of the relevant information and connections that were encountered. A new approach is required to handle such fragmented information, to discover the relevant facts, and to deal with the phenomenon of everything getting more interrelated.

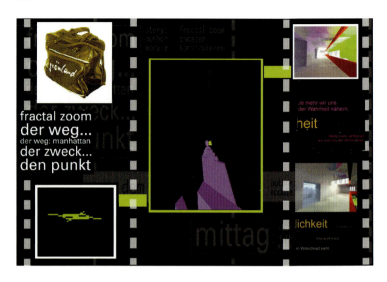

The Aus dem Punkt gebracht *node as a connection between the stories* Fractal Zoom *and* Jenseits, *node by Matthias Brühlmann and Christoph Lötscher. Composition by MMB.*

Reading a hyperdocument differs from linear media not only because of interconnection, since semiotics also have an extra dimension. The same piece of information can have different meanings depending on the context in which it is encountered. The authors of a hyperdocument have less control over the context and the possible interpretations of their writing than the authors of linear media. It may be

impossible to foresee all the possible paths that lead to one piece of information. Our experience has shown that there are qualities that are independent of the context. Some bits of information unfold brilliantly in whatever circumstances they are encountered.

73

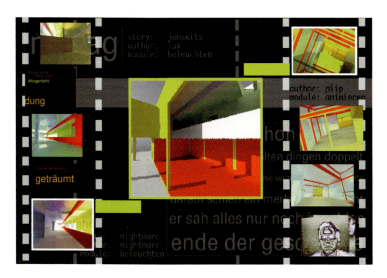

Warm, *a new node between the stories* Jenseits *and* Nightmare, *node by Rahel Marti and Gabriela Eichenberger. Composition by MMB.*

Orientation is another challenge to both the reader and the writer. It is almost impossible to know how much one has already read of a hyperdocument and how much one still has to go. This is different from a book, where progress can be measured by comparing the thickness of the part that has been read with the unread part. It is impossible to browse quickly in a linear fashion through a hyperdocument and revise the information at a very high speed. To retrieve a certain passage in a hypertext, either the path to get there has to be remembered or special retrieval mechanisms have to be provided. Solutions to this aspect will be presented in the next chapter, when highly interrelated infor-

mation is regarded as an information space that allows a variety of different views.
Hypertext reading and writing, as well as the aspect of orientation, are overwhelmingly challenging at first and time and cultural adjustment will be needed for the whole of society to achieve a real hyperdocument literacy.

7. Information Spaces: New Spheres to Explore

Information spaces are formations that can not be grasped easily in their entirety. Information spaces are dynamically changing multidimensional digital buildings. The digital data can be formed and structured, meaning and purpose can be added, and multiple dimensions can be introduced. The material – the raw mass of information – has to be turned into architecture. The purpose of this architecture is to make information accessible by converting it into a form that motivates the visitor to engage in exploration. The design ambitions of digital architecture will be as high as for physical architecture. Although the circumstances and the means of expression differ considerably, the goal is to meet high standards regarding form, function, and aesthetics.

Physical Architecture has evolved over many centuries, thereby gaining more and more complexity. It began with single room dwellings often symbolized by Laugier's primitive hut. Today it has reached the point where buildings can even react to their environment like the *Tower of winds* by Toy Ito. Information architecture – in its infancy as a design field – already has to deal with enormous complexity. This stems from the multifaceted nature of the medium on the one hand, and from expectations which are far ahead of the solutions on the other. There are many assumptions regarding what computers should be able to do and as many frustrations because they cannot do it yet. Nonetheless, most computer users are not aware of the missing aesthetics in their digital environments and how they could facilitate the work on a computer. The Mac interface is a nice example of how the elegance of the interface (see Saggio, 1998) and the underlying structure of the computer hardware can enhance the usability. Before 1984, computers were mostly used by specialists and

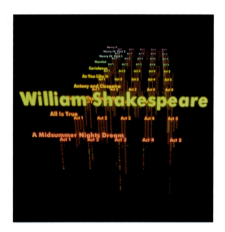 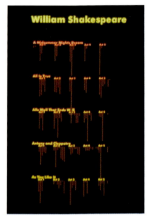

Navigating large amounts of Text *a model of the entire plays of Shakespeare, where one can move from a view of the whole oeuvre to the single word. Project by David Small (Copyright MIT Media Lab, 1995).*

laypersons had little chance of understanding the machine, because all commands had to be typed in using a special language. Then the Mac interface (originally developed at Xerox) offered an easy way of understanding what the computer can do. The desktop metaphor allowed the capabilities of the machine to be explored without prior knowledge and attracted a new sort of computer user. It was not only the visible part that was revolutionary, but the whole computer architecture had a new, elegant structure that supported a seamless interaction between human and computer.

The Mac interface has influenced many of the well known user-interfaces, but the next revolution of the interface is coming. Ideas about the next user-interfaces, which may leave more autonomy to the computer, can be found in the article "The Anti-Mac Interface" by Don Gentner and Jakob Nielson. (Genter, Nielson, 1996).

Views

A hyperdocument – a collection of linked information nodes – forms a structure, so that every piece of information can be accessed in at least one way. Such an information space is multidimensional, since there are many different aspects that can serve as coordinates. When represented on a screen, it is reduced to two dimensions. Whether this is a projection of a three-dimensional representation or a precisely generated two-dimensional image is not a primary concern. In the search for the appropriate form for the representation, important questions are: Which aspects should be emphasized? What information should be shown at what point in time? Which dynamics will be useful to explore the information space? What kind of creative interaction will be helpful? Architecture in the digital realm, in addition to providing a space for information, also means creating the views that help to understand the content, structure, and dynamics.

The entire plays of Shakespeare have been visualized as one information space by David Small at

the Visible Language Workshop (Small, 1996). The three-dimensional structure allows readers to zoom from an overview to the single word. By changing the scale, different aspects of the plays can be studied. The first level shows the impressive universe of Shakespearean plays, titles can be seen in relation to the length of the pieces. On a next level, it is possible to focus on a single play and see the structure of the text as well as the interplay of different characters through color-coding. Monologues, dialogues, and scenes with multiple players become visually apparent. The Shakespeare example shows a pre-calculated model that is not reconfigured during interaction. Its quality lies in the careful display of information on every scale. It is most important that the color value and the form of the paragraphs remain constant. This requires the development of sophisticated algorithms to generate the views on the different scales.

Zooming is a way to create views with different semantic content. Calculated views can be used to generate different thematic content. *Fake.space*, *phase(X)*, and *Multiplying Time* (discussed in Schmitt, 1998) make a distinction between private inworld and public outworld views. An inworld view presents an individual, subjective, limited framework for navigation within the space. An outworld view is an objective overview onto the information space that makes relations between smaller information entities apparent. Every information space should offer to provide connections between inworld and outworld views.

The Shakespeare example allows a smooth transition from outworld to inworld, while the other examples create various outworld views with many links to the inworlds. Each outworld view focuses on a specific aspect of the information space. *Fake.space*'s text-based outworld is called map. It shows different categories of contributions: the newest, the most visited, special categories, and thematic lists. *Fake.space*'s graphical

outworld is called sky. It shows how the system has grown outwards from the central connector. In *phase(X)* graphs about the system get calculated to show the exchange of ideas between different contributions. There are also 3D views that show more complex relations, for example between time, quality, and the author of each piece of work in the space. The interesting aspect about providing different views onto a space is that they allow multiple levels of reading. The RAMA-view (named after a spaceship in Clark, 1990) was created for the courses on *Raumgeschichten* (single stories) and *Hyperräume* (interconnected stories). The cylindrical form shows the stories on the outside, and inside the different connections created with new nodes and movies.

Activities
Reading is a space-creating activity. Through the act of reading, we merge the separate scenes into a continuous space that exists only in our minds (Murray, 1997, p. 110).

> This space is perceived through motion, physical or mental movements. The space in which we move has its own structure as it is available to us. In its action on us, space will be loaded with meaning as a place of return, or it will evade us, opposing itself to us. (Lischka, 1997, p. 129)

An information space is a space where information is made accessible, where one can acquire knowledge and find answers. The digital environment allows for engaging and motivating interactions. Travelling along various paths in a hyperdocument, and exploring relations in different views were mentioned earlier. Other possibilities for interactions are the gathering, filtering, and sorting of information. However, the most intriguing way of using the information is to create new meaning.

The nodes in our environments have an interesting semantic poten-

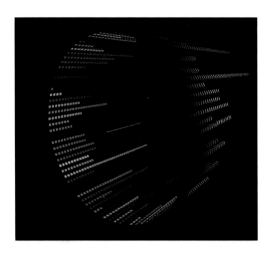

The RAMA outworld view. The stories are represented around a cylindric form.

tial. Depending on the sequence in which a node is encountered, it can mean something different. Image-nodes have an even bigger range of possible interpretations than text-nodes. Information spaces have similar characteristics to languages. The vocabulary is given through the nodes. By introducing new connections, new sentences can be formed, thereby composing a message that was not part of the space before and broadening the knowledge contained in it. Examples of such creative activities have been implemented in our environments. A person who knows the information in the system can think of a new theme and search for a sequence of nodes to illustrate it. In the course on *Hyperräume*, such new sequences are called movies, because the result creates the structure for a new movement through the information space.

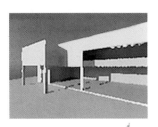

Attention and Enjoyment

Attention is the most precious commodity in a worldwide network like the Internet. Space is limitless, speed is increasing, and functionality is improving, the most scarce resource is human attention (see Goldhaber, 1997).

Connections between stories are shown inside. The 3D model is always interactively calculated and represents the actual state. Programming and design by Patrick Sibenaler.

Everyone lives a 24-hour day and has many things to do, the time spent online is limited. If we publish information online we first have to attract the readers' attention and then we need the means to keep it.

Hypertext Gardens by Mark Bernstein (http://www.eastgate.com/garden/) is a particularly appealing example of hypertext. Bernstein explores how architecture and landscape design might guide us in crafting hypertexts. In the introduction he writes: "The time, care, and expense devoted to creating and promoting a hypertext are lost if readers arrive, glance around, and click elsewhere" (Bernstein).

Many beliefs about the design of hyperdocuments are questioned. This is necessary, because there are many sterile, simplistic websites that are designed according to basic assumptions and a naïve selection of rules. Often websites are structured according to a strict hierarchy, with the result that one has to click through five pages to get to the desired information. On all the four pages in-between there was probably nothing of current interest to the visitor. A different

approach is taken when designing a hypertext like a garden. It allows irregularities within the concept. It emphasizes that joy is an important part of the experience and that the pace of travelling can differ: a pause is sometimes needed, at other times one might like to run around.

It took fifty years of experimentation and more to establish such conventions as legible typefaces, page numbering, paragraphing, title pages, prefaces, chapter divisions, which together make the published book a coherent means of communication (Murray, 1997, p. 28). We are in the middle of a similar process of discovering writing in the digital era. There is much left to discover. We still have to be inventive. Using the metaphors of the older media is a clear indication that the new medium is not used to its full potential yet. The search for the appropriate expressive means for this new medium, made possible by engineers and computer scientists, poses an intriguing challenge for architects, designers, artists, as well as philosophers.

8. Learning: Discoveries Beyond the Frontier

To tackle new challenges, to explore new possibilities and to step beyond what is currently possible and acceptable in architectural practice are prerequisites in the search for answers to the question: How can architecture be revealed on a screen? The goals for learning go even further than the answer to this question.

Learning has to be a Fun, Creative, Social and Cultural Activity

Learning is a walk on the border between being entertaining and leading to measurable progress. This border is widening and creating room where work and play, learning and fun, information and entertainment overlap. With the fast pace of changes in our environment every person will have to constantly learn new things for the rest of their lives. It is therefore important to discover joyful personal learning methods. We have difficulty remembering abstract knowledge, but we can more easily remember a good story (Schank, 1990, p. 10). This was also realized by Marvin Minsky, a famous Artificial Intelligence expert and author of the book *Society of Minds*. In order to make the theory of the Society of Minds more widely understandable he wrote a science fiction novel *The Touring Option* together with the science fiction author Harry Harrison. The narrative form has the advantage that it is entertaining and every reader can find an individual access to the described events.

Learning is a creative process. The brain receives information and has to store it so that it will be useful in the future. The process of storing information means that relations to already available knowledge have to be established in the brain. Reading as well as writing stories deepens one's knowledge and the experience becomes part of one's memories.

The Last Frames - *A small collection of endings of stories.*

Therefore, reading as well as writing provokes a creative learning process.

Learning is a cultural process. By comparing the common sense of today's generation to the common sense of people of the last century, it becomes obvious that collective, cultural learning processes are taking place. This is only possible through the exchange of ideas. Therefore, communication is a fundamental mechanism for learning and the cultural development of a society. Kevin Kelly calls it coevolution:

In the Networked Era – that age we have just entered – dense communication is creating artificial worlds ripe for emergent coevolution, spontaneous self-organization, and win-win cooperation. In this Era, openness wins, central control is lost, and stability is a state of perpetual almost-falling ensured by constant error. (Kelly, 1994, p. 90)

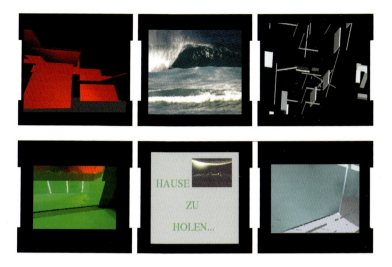

Architecture, Computers and Learning
Every design task asks for an invention, a solution to answer the needs defined by the client and the circumstances. Therefore, learning has to focus on three aspects: observing, judging, and inventing. It is an important ability for architects and creative workers to be able to judge designs. During a design process, numerous solutions are generated and the act of selecting the right one is as important as their generation.

> Designers frequently recognize emergent subshapes and subsequently structure their understanding of the design and their reasoning about it in terms of emergent entities and relationships. (Mitchell, 1989)

For the creation, the communication and the formulation of architecture it is necessary that architects know as much as possible about the potential of computers, networks, and the use of the new medium. However, the tools per

se are not the issue, but the possibilities, the spirit, and the effects of the new medium. The attitude should be similar to that used when selecting building materials for a design. For example, concrete can be used to build carefully modelled forms. To design these forms, an architect does not have to be able to build them, but needs to have enough understanding of the material and the building process to be able to create an appropriate design, a design that can be built and will result in the desired effect. The process also happens the other way around; an architect may first know the effect that he would like to achieve and has to search for the appropriate material. When trying to use the computer in the design process, it is important to know about the possibilities and integrate the computer accordingly.

How can the possibilities of a medium be learned if it is still evolving? One has to think in dynamic terms. Explorations beyond what is currently known will help to establish a dynamic future-oriented process. Again, we can find a parallel in architecture, where styles evolve according to new influences and insights that question the current practice. Such processes, as well as discussions about the consequences have to be initiated at university level.

For courses at a university level, as well as for life as an architect, it is not efficient to focus learning on single computer programs. This has been proven in our courses. In the courses *Raumgeschichten* and *Hyperräume* the learning of programs happened almost as a side-effect. The students learned to model, render, animate, to write HTML code, to use image and sound processing driven by the goal to write a story. Just to learn a program does not offer enough academic themes to discuss and can be quite boring. On the other hand, writing a story really leads to new thoughts and questions about the project on hand and architecture in general. In both cases, you learn to master new programs, but when writing stories everything that is learned in addition to the programs

makes it an exciting learning experience. To count the tools that one has learned is easy. To find out about the knowledge that was acquired is rather more difficult, but can be evaluated. However, the most important issue and the hardest to measure, is the experience that was gained. Today's computer programs are going to change. Today's knowledge about computers will become less important, because the interfaces are going to integrate much of this knowledge so that the user can focus better on the task-related issues. Experience, after all, is the foundation to build upon. Don't dissect a frog, build one (Negroponte, 1995, p. 199).

To focus on the architectural issues when working on the computer is very important. Thinking about the tools is necessary but secondary with respect to the desired product, namely the building, with its character, atmosphere, and beauty. Having the architectural goal in mind helps you to stay focused when working with a medium, where the possibilities can be overwhelming. The goal helps to choose the tools from a range that is growing daily. The goal helps to guide exploration of the new medium that is full of secret possibilities.

Narratives, Networks and Architecture
Digital Stories and *Hyperspaces* were chosen as themes for our courses to search for ways to reveal architectonic ideas with the computer. The courses went beyond this main intention in many ways.

Much will change in the coming years and decades in the field of architecture. There is a newly discovered territory to be conquered. There is an information space in need of an architecture, a media space, where the possibilities of the medium still need to be discovered, a digital space, that will influence our physical architecture in many ways. It will change the way architecture is created, the design communicated, and it is already becoming more and more part of our built architecture. The digital and the physical architecture are merging.

88

Sad Story by Andrew vande Moere, making the best out of data loss and other problems with the computer and the network, this story is an amusing show of the struggle with the machine. Composition by MMB.

The new territory enabled by the World Wide Web is an extraordinary chance to learn how to explore something new and to invent new uses.

Students and professors, practitioners and philosophers are participating in the same progressing field. An ideal situation for learners, because they can observe the experts and support them with own ideas. Shared exploration is challenging for teachers. They

have to be facilitators instead of knowledge providers and they have to mediate a process instead of delivering information, which requires excellent judgmental and creative abilities.

To write a story requires a design process. How does this process relate to the architectural design process? Can the writing of a story influence the design of a space? The writing of stories influences our thinking. While writing stories about a project, the creative aspect of learning can feed back into the design. Writing can become part of the design process,

which requires the introduction of imaginative events and fictitious explorations of the virtually created spaces to evaluate its validity. Every version of a story changes our perception of the room. The intensity of analysis needed to write a story will result in questions regarding the design and it may also lead to new solutions, because of the changed focus. In a story, some aspects will be clearer than in plans, models and other representations. There may be surprises for the designer, which, if interpreted honestly, will be good indicators for the quality of the work. Stories will not only help to communicate but also to improve a design.

Digital Environments for Learning
The architecture of the learning environment influences the quality of learning. The environments have to create a space for the collaborative exploration of ideas. The networked environments are designed for learning but also integrate the aspect of computer-supported collaborative work, an additional aspect that was experienced by the students that worked in our environments. They learned to use the contributions of others creatively, they learned to share their own ideas and find new ways of identifying with their work, and they learned to take responsibility for the environment they are taking part of.

> As the audience becomes a participant in the total electric drama, the classroom can become a scene in which the audience performs an enormous amount of work. (McLuhan, 1967, p. 101)

To enable a creative atmosphere in an "electronic classroom",

special attention has to be paid to motivation, transparency, and support. Motivation means providing interesting themes, challenges, and rewarding situations. Transparency means making the work in the whole environment visible and useable. Transparency supports the spreading of ideas, it may help students in situations where they are stuck without an idea. Students learn a lot by looking at each other's work, because they can compare different solutions to the same task and they will inevitably learn to judge what they see. A supportive environment is a well-designed environment, where one can feel secure and comfortable. It contains all the information needed to fulfil the tasks technically and it supports the navigation through its space with different views, so that users and visitors always find interesting aspects to explore.

Stories are a medium for communication, learning, and design. Digital Stories enhance these qualities, with the numerous possibilities of the information processing machine and its connection to the global communication network.

Bibliography

Bear, G., *EON*, Tom Doherty Assocs. Inc., New York 1985.

Bernstein, M., *Hypertextgardens*, http://www.eastgate.com/garden/.

Bush, V., *As We May Think*, reprinted in *From Memex to Hypertext*, J, Nyce, P. Kahn, eds., Academic Press, Cambridge, MA 1991, pp. 85–110.

Calvino, I., *Invisible Cities*, Harcourt Brace, New York 1986.

Clark, A.Ch., *Rendezvous with Rama*, Bantam Books, New York 1990.

Cooper M., Small D., *Visible Language Workshop in Information Architects*, R. S. Wurman, Ed., Graphis Press Corp., Zürich 1996, pp. 202–211.

Cummings Loud, P., *The Art Museums of Louis I. Kahn*, Duke University Press, Durham 1989.

Eisner, W., *Comics and Sequential Art*, Poorhouse Press, Florida 1985.

Goldhaber, M.H., "Attention Shoppers!", in *WIRED*, San Francisco, Issue 5.12, December, 1997.

Gentner D., Nielson T., "The Anti-Mac Interface", in *Communications of the ACM*, Volume 39, no. 8, New York 1996, pp. 70–82.

Greenberg, Saul, *Lecture on Graphical Screen Design*, http://www.cpsc.ucalgary.ca/-grouplab/people/saul/hci_topics/topics/grapical_design.

Johnson, N.E., *Light is the Theme: Louis I. Kahn and the Kimbell Art Museum*, Kimbell Art Foundation, Fort Worth 1975.

Kahle, B., "Archiving the Internet", in *Scientific American*, November 4, 1996.

Kelly, K., *Out of Control*, Addison Wesley, Reading, MA 1994.

Kishi, W., "Waro Kishi", in *El Croquis*, 1996, 77, Madrid 1996.

Laurel, B., *Computers as Theater*, Addison Wesley Publishing Company, Reading, MA 1991.

Lebrande, S., *Example-Based Character Drawing*, Master Thesis, MIT Media Lab, 1993.

Lischka, J.G., *Johann Gerhard, Schnittstellen – Das postmoderne Weltbild*, Benteli Verlag, 1997.

McCloud, S., *Understanding Comics*, Kitchen Sink Press, Northampton, MA 1993.

McLuhan, M., Fiore, Q., *The Medium is the Message*, 1967, renewed 1996 by Jerome Agel, Hardwired, San Francisco 1996.

Mitchell, W.J., *The Logic of Architecture*, MIT Press, Cambridge 1990.

Munsell, A.H., *A Color Notation*, Munsell Color Company, Baltimore, MD 1923.

Murray, J.H., *Hamlet on the Holodeck – The Future of Narrative in Cyberspace*, The Free Press, New York 1997.

Negroponte, N., *Being Digital*, Vintage Books, New York 1995.

Saggio, A., *Afterword* in Prestinenza Puglisi, L., *HyperArchitecture*, Birkhäuser, Basel 1999.

Schank, R., *Tell Me a Story – Narrative and Intelligence*, 1990, Northwestern University Press, Illinois 1995.

Schmitt, G., *Information Architecture*, Birkhäuser, Basel 1999.

Small, D., "Navigating Large Bodies of Text", in *IBM Systems Journal*, Vol. 35, 1996, p. 514–526.

Trabant, J., *Vicos Welt-Schrift*, in S. Krämer, P. Koch (eds.), *Schrift, Medien, Kognition – Über die Exteriorität des Geistes*, p. 149–166, *Probleme der Semiotik*, no. 19, Stauffenburg Verlag, Germany, 1997.

Tschumi, B., *Architecture and Disjunction*, MIT Press, Cambridge, MA 1994.

Tufte, E., *The Visual Display of Quantitative Information*, Graphics Press, Chesrie, CN 1985.

Turkle, S., *Life Behind the Screen – Identity in the Age of the Internet*, Simon & Schuster, New York 1995.

Wenz F., Gramazio F., *Archaeology of the Future City: TRACE*, in Schmitt G. *Architektur mit dem Computer*, Vieweg, Wiesbaden 1996, p. 177–179.

Wolf, G., "The Curse of Xanadu", in *WIRED*, 3.06, June, 1995.

Wurman, R.S., *Information Architects*, Graphis Press Corp., Zürich 1996.

Wingler, H.M., *Das Bauhaus*, MIT Press, Cambridge, MA 1969.

INTERNET SITES

Absolut Vodka: http://www.absolutvodka.com/
The Internet Archive: http://www.archive.org/
The Kimbell Art Museum: http://www.kimbellart.org/
Raumgeschichten, Hyperräume: http://alterego.arch.ethz.ch/
virtualhouse.ch: http://virtualhouse.ch/

The Information Technology Revolution in Architecture is a new series reflecting on the effects the virtual dimension is having on architects and architecture in general. Each volume will examine a single topic, highlighting the essential aspects and exploring their relevance for the architects of today.

Series edited by **Antonino Saggio**

Other titles in this series:

Information Architecture
Basis and future of CAAD
Gerhard Schmitt
ISBN 3-7643-6092-5

HyperArchitecture
Spaces in the Electronic Age
Luigi Prestinenza Puglisi
ISBN 3-7643-6093-3

Digital Eisenman
An Office of the Electronic Era
Luca Galofaro
ISBN 3-7643-6094-1

Virtual Terragni
CAAD in Historical and Critical Research
Mirko Galli / Claudia Mühlhoff
ISBN 3-7643-6174-3

Natural Born CAADesigners
Young American Architects
Christian Pongratz / Maria Rita Perbellini
ISBN 3-7643-6246-4

For our free catalog please contact:

Birkhäuser – Publishers for Architecture
P. O. Box 133, CH-4010 Basel, Switzerland
Tel. ++41-(0)61-205 07 07; Fax ++41-(0)61-205 07 92
e-mail: sales@birkhauser.ch
http://www.birkhauser.ch